VO₂ MAX

VO$_2$ MAX

Athlete's Journal

Richard Kent, Ph.D.

Dedication:

For my nephew, Fred... gifted athlete, wonderful man.

Acknowledgments:

My thanks to the many writers, athletes, and coaches who have guided my thinking about athletic team notebooks and journals. I am indebted to Sam Morse of Carrabassett Valley Academy who shared his extensive journals and good thoughts. Gayle Sirois provided feedback, encouragement, and her editor's eye all while setting a 1500-mile *PR* in 2012.

NATIONAL WRITING PROJECT

This book is published in cooperation with the National Writing Project, University of California, 2105 Bancroft Way, Berkeley, CA 94720

CONTENTS

WRITING YOUR GAME

"We write not to say what we know, but to learn, to discover, to know."
–Donald Murray

U.S. ski racer Sam Morse has been keeping journals for 9 years. At 16-years old, Sam has filled a slew of black-marble composition books and 3-ring binders with notes, reflections, and the stuff of his impressive ski-racing career. "Writing for me is a way to process what is buzzing around in my head," he said. "When I put my thoughts on paper, I begin to see things more clearly." Sam's not alone.

Athletic greats like Serena Williams and Michael Phelps keep journals. So did baseball superstars Carlos Delgado and Curt Schilling. In England, 16- to 18-year-old apprentices to professional soccer teams write journals about their games, training sessions, and health. American athletes in schools and colleges use team notebooks to reflect on the previous season, to set goals, and to analyze a game or performance.

Sport psychologists work with most college and professional athletic teams. They have athletes write as a way to look more closely at their training and competitions, and to resolve issues like anxiety or fear of failure. Writing also complements other techniques like meditation and visualization.

And sometimes athletes just write on their own because of an innate need to think more deeply about their sport, to work things out, and to tell their stories. To understand that, think about the reasons so many of us blog, Facebook, or Tweet.

There are countless ways to improve as an athlete; writing is one of them. "We write not to say what we know," said Pulitzer Prize winner Donald Murray, "but to learn, to discover, to know." This is to say that writing is a powerful way to learn, and that's why scientists, historians, and even Wimbledon tennis champions keep notebooks. As William Zinsser explained:

> "Writing organizes and clarifies our thoughts. Writing is how we think our way into a subject and make it our own. Writing enables us to find out what we know—and what we don't know—about whatever we're trying to learn."

Sport psychologists have long understood that writing can also affect an athlete's physical and emotional well being by

- reducing stress and anxiety,
- increasing self-awareness,
- sharpening mental skills,
- promoting psychological insight, and
- strengthening coping abilities.

Take a second look at this list above. Could working on these issues help you move to the next level as an athlete? If so, writing can play a role.

The Basics

This book includes 72 journal prompts that will help you think more specifically about your training, competitions, and life as an athlete. Following the athlete's journals, you'll find *pre- mid- and postseason* reflections. The prompts on these pages will guide your thinking before, during, and after your competitive season. Finally, the pages of Competition Analyses will lead you to unpack this season's competitions.

Most of the prompts are known as *quick writes* and can be accomplished in 3-5 minutes. When you begin writing, try not to stop. Keep your pen or pencil on the paper and just keep writing. If your mind goes blank, make a list of words related to the topic until you start composing sentences again. If you run out of space and have more to say, continue writing on the additional blank journal pages provided at the back of the book. And please don't be overly concerned about the conventions of writing like spelling, grammar, or paragraphing. Just write.

And finally

Writing in a notebook isn't going to replace organized training or good coaching. No athlete is going to immediately score more points, win more medals, or raise their VO_2 Max because of journals. However, if what the experts say about writing is even marginally true—that it could help you learn more or reduce stress—wouldn't these potential benefits be worth a few of minutes of writing every day or so?

In sport, victories are often achieved by inches or in hundredths of seconds after many hours of training. To advance your game, add a few words to your day, and see where they take you.

Richard Kent
Orono, Maine

ATHLETE'S JOURNALS

1.

At this moment in your career, what's your primary quality as an athlete? When asked to name a strength, some athletes identified the following:

Focused	Cardio	Dedicated	Fit
Confident	Competitive	Motivated	Brave
Leader	Unshakable	Positive	Skillful
Hardworking	Fearless	Tenacity	Strong

Write about your primary quality or strength as an athlete...

2.

Who brings out the best in you as an athlete and why? You might first think of a coach, manager, or trainer. But also think about family members, friends, fans, teammates, or even an opponent.

3.

Mental Imagery: Think back and recall your best moments as an athlete. Remember the exact details of a perfect pass, brilliant move, or powerful run. Make a list of those moments and create your own mental performance video that you can play back to yourself as preparation for a game or practice, or to use during a competition to gain back confidence. Your mental performance video might last between 10-30 seconds.

Example Image: In the soccer game against Telstar HS, I ran the ball down the touchline into the attacking third. As the goalkeeper came out, I touched a beautiful ball over his head to the far post for a score. I remember the way the ball felt on my foot.

Image:

Image:

Image:

Image:

Image:

4.

Write about one of your favorite teammates,
training partners, or opponents.

Name or initials: _____

Qualities as an athlete:

Qualities as a person:

Unique habits or quirks:

A story you'd share about this athlete:

What have you learned from this athlete?

More:

5.

Make a list of five qualities you believe an effective coach must have. Give an example from a coach you know.

Quality _____:

Quality _____:

Quality _____:

Quality _____:

Quality _____:

6.

Think about one area in your sport that you'd like to improve upon. Use an Internet search engine like Google and find a video on that subject. Watch the video and write about the following:

Title of Video: _____

–What new information did you learn?

–What might you try out or how might you adapt your play?

–What questions did you have after watching the video?

–What ideas might you share with a fellow athlete?

–What knowledge might you share with your coach?

–What suggestions might you make for revising this video:

7.

What makes training hard for you?

What makes training easy for you?

8.

Write your response and a reason why:

My favorite training food is . . .

During a competition I am nervous about . . .

My favorite exercise or activity during a training session is . . .

When I hear _____ from an opponent or an opponent's fan, I feel like . . .

When my team or I win a competition by a wide margin, I . . .

When my coach says _____ I feel like . . .

9.

Other than winning a competition, tell the story of your proudest moment as an athlete.

10.

Watch your sport on television or listen on the radio… make a list of some the announcer's best descriptive lines.

11.

Write a letter to one of your former coaches. You may wish to include: what you're doing now as an athlete; the coach's contributions to your life; the issues you currently face as an athlete; a fun memory; a photo. You may wish to mail a revised version of the letter to your former coach.

12.

"Some days, playing poorly is the most important result that could happen." Give an example from your own experience as an athlete why can this statement be true.

13.

How do you learn your sport? Look at this figure and circle the ways you learn as an athlete.

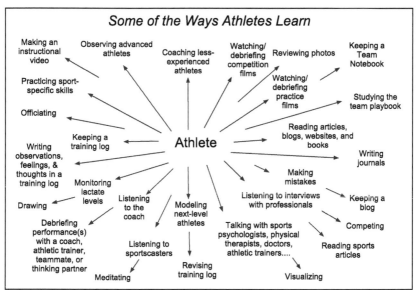

Reprinted with permission, *Writing on the Bus* (Kent, 2012, p. 14)

Picking from the various learning activities above, what could you add to your own experience to help you improve as an athlete? Explain.

Are there ways you learn that are not included in the figure above? List them below.

14.

Describe your most humiliating experience as an athlete. What might you have learned from this experience?

15.

Select one or more of the terms and write in the space at the right:

Poor sport

Great eye

A good loss

Future star

Miscommunication

Injury

Suck-up

Cheat

Focus

Training

Fitness

Teammate

Official

Coach

Trainer

Foul

Frightened

Technical

Discipline

Reward

Practice

16.

Using your most recent competition, respond to the following:

–Describe the evening before this competition. Did you prepare the way you should have?

–On game day, how did you spend your time? Did you eat/hydrate adequately? If you could improve one aspect of your preparation for this competition, what would it be?

–Describe your pre-game preparation (e.g., warm-up). Is there any aspect of your pre-game that you'd improve upon?

–Describe your mindset <u>during</u> the competition. Were you focused and motivated?

–Describe your post-game recovery. Did you stretch, hydrate, and eat appropriately? Is there any aspect of your post-game that you'd change?

17.

There are times just before a competition when you feel "on." You're ready to have at it and everything is in sync. Other days… not so much. Why is that? What specific "things" affect your performance as an athlete? Could it be friends, sleep, food, the opponent, your coach, your mood, or even the wrong socks? Make two lists of what may influence your performances, even in the smallest ways, during a competition.

Good Performance	Bad Performance
Sample: I knew my opponent.	*Sample: I lacked confidence*

What comes to mind when you think about the lists above?

18.

If you're a natural athlete, describe what it's like to someone who is not. If you're not a natural athlete, write about what it's like to train with or compete against someone who is. If you are a natural athlete, what's your biggest frustration. If you are not, why has that been a good thing for you?

19.

Maybe you've done some coaching and officiating in your sport. Maybe not. Write about the following prompts:

–What are the most challenging aspects of being a coach in your sport?

–What are the most challenging aspects of being an official in your sport?

20.

Who is the oldest athlete you know. Describe the athlete. What characteristics of this person do you admire?

21.

Describe your earliest memory as an athlete.

22.

If you could relive one moment as an athlete, what would it be and why would you want to go back?

23.

Tell the story about a time as an athlete that you quit. It might have been giving up during a training session or a competition. It may have been as big as walking out on your team or as small as you stopped listening to your coach during a halftime talk.

As you look back at this time, what might you do differently if this happened now?

24.

What is something you dislike about yourself as an athlete?

25.

Think back to a time when an athlete or team you supported lost big-time in a competition that they were favored to win. Describe your feelings.

26.

Picture a younger athlete who admires you. How would they describe you as an athlete and as a person.

27.

In sports, there are things we can control and things we can't. For example, we can't control the weather, our coach's decisions, or what someone says about us. We can control the amount of sleep we get, the volume and quality of training we do, the diet we maintain, and the attitude we bring to a practice or competition. Write about a time when you let something you could <u>not</u> control get the better of you. What happened? How did you react? What would you do now under the same circumstances?

28.

Make a list of five good things that are happening in your life right now outside of sport. Select one or two and write about them.

1. _____

2. _____

3. _____

4. _____

5. _____

29.

How do you prepare for a game or competition? Many athletes have routines that they follow. They may go to bed at a certain time, eat specific foods, listen to particular music, or talk with certain people. Some athletes review their own "game plans" and, using mental imagery, "watch" their mental performance video. Write about your pre-competition routine. If you have not established one or wish to revise the one you have, write about that.

30.

Make a list of what you say to yourself during a competition. You may well want to write down this "self talk" just after a game or competition. This internal dialog may include feelings ("We're going to destroy this team."), instructions you give yourself ("Hang back! Hang back! Wait until she makes her move."), or random thoughts ("What did that fan just say to Alex?")

31.

Read through your list of "self talk" on the previous page and write about what you notice. Is your talk positive, instructive, and motivating? Do you spend too much time complaining about a teammate, the coach, or an official? In the end, you'll want to decide whether your talk is productive or destructive, positive or negative, or informative or unhelpful.

32.

Make a list of the most negative or nastiest things you've heard during a practice or game. Select one of them and write about it.

33.

This page is for your coach, a teammate, an opponent,
an official, or anyone who knows you as an athlete.

Instructions: Please take a few minutes to write about this athlete. You might comment on the athlete's attitude, focus, skills, athleticism, fitness, work ethic, dedication, confidence, or leadership. There's more room at the back of the journal if you need it.

34.

Read the previous entry and write your reaction to the person's comments.

35.

What is your favorite place to compete and why?

36.

Throughout your time as an athlete, you have discovered some favorite resources that you've used to expand your knowledge and enjoyment of your sport. Make a list of some of the websites, YouTube videos, books, magazines, Facebook pages, or movies that you would recommend to a younger athlete.

37.

What is a good opponent?

38.

After a competition, write a performance analysis of a teammate or fellow athlete. What did you notice about the athlete's strengths? What advice would you give to this athlete?

39.

Henry David Thoreau wrote, "Less is more." Sometimes distilling our stories is a perfect way to see our athletic lives more clearly. Try to write some six-word sports stories about your training, team, or a recent game. Here's an example from a hockey playoff game: "Into OT— Hail Mary empty netter."

40.

Write about an athlete who is a "poser." Why do you think this happens to some athletes? When, if ever, have you come close to being a poser? Why do you think it happened to you?

41.

What advice or talk do you <u>least</u> like to hear before an important game or competition? Why?

42.

Describe an athlete you would never want to be a teammate with.

43.

What's the best competition you've ever seen in person? Describe the details and explain what made it *the best*.

44.

Draw a picture of your favorite piece of sports equipment and write one sentence about it.

45.

Write about the kindest thing you have ever done as an athlete.

46.

After a game or match, write a letter to the opposing coach. What positive things would you say to this coach? Would you have any suggestions? How about questions? This isn't a letter you're going to send; it's just way to think more deeply about your opponent. If you come to know your opponent more fully, you'll come to know yourself more completely, too.

47.

It's often said that we are who we spend the most time with. Who are the five people, athletes or not, that you spend the most time with? In what ways do they affect who you are?

48.

We are our thoughts and actions. In the callout below, list the <u>individual</u> words (not phrases or sentences) that are upper most in your mind and that represent you as both athlete and person.

49.

Make a list of your favorite "things" in your sport. They could be plays, equipment, moments, places, or people. Page back through this journal as a way to recall some of your favorites. An example? The moment after a sudden death, overtime win.

50.

Finish this sentence: I deserve a day off from training because…

51.

Make a list of the people, athletes or not, that you would stand in a very long line to meet. What do these people have in common? What does this list say about you?

52.

Draw a sketch of where you compete—e.g., a pool, field, track, course, rink, half-pipe, road, jump, court, and arena. Now label different places on the drawing where something memorable happened.

53.

Definition of envy: painful or resentful awareness of an advantage enjoyed by another joined with a desire to possess the same advantage.

Whom do you envy as an athlete? What specifically do you envy about this person? How could you possess the advantage they seem to have?

54.

Who do you think envies you as an athlete? What do they see in you that is enviable?

55.

What would you do differently if you could have a "do-over" in your last game or competition?

56.

After a competition, write a note to one of your opponents. Perhaps it's an athlete that you played against directly—e.g., guarded in basketball, challenged in tennis, ran against in a race—or someone you watched on defense while you played offense.

57.

Describe the last time you lost your cool in a competition. How did it affect your play? Did anyone say anything to you? What did you learn from this experience?

58.

Write from the perspective of your youngest competitive self about the athlete you have become. Begin with this opening:

Dear _____,

When I was ____ *years old, I dreamed about being an older athlete like you are now. I thought that I would be* _____.
Now, I am ...

59.

Tell the story of when your mind really let you down as an athlete.

60.

Attach a photograph of yourself in the space below.

What would people be surprised to know after looking at this photograph?

61.

Think back through your athletic career and make a list of the teams you've played on or the age levels you competed at. What did you learn? Who do you remember from those days?

Team/Age Group_____:

Team/Age Group_____:

Team/Age Group_____:

Team/Age Group_____:

Team/Age Group_____:

Team/Age Group_____:

Team/Age Group_____:

62.

What special story would you like told at a sports banquet or in a newspaper/magazine about a teammate, coach, fan, or opponent and why?

63.

Throughout an athletic season you experience highs and lows, ups and downs. Think back through the season and give examples of the following:

I laughed…

I cried or got emotional…

I screamed like a wild person…

I got crazy angry…

I sat and stared in disbelief…

I just didn't care…

I wanted to hide…

I wanted someone to see…

64.

Find a favorite newspaper article about your team, a fellow athlete, your season, or you. If you or your team didn't make the newspapers, look through Facebook or a blog post for a favorite comment. Write about what has been written.

65.

Make a list of 10 quotations by athletes in your sport. You may find lists of quotations by athletes by searching the Web.

66.

Select your favorite quotation from the list on the previous page and write about it.

67.

Tell about a time when you were genuinely happy for another athlete's poor performance or loss.

68.

In your opinion, who is the best athlete in your sport today? Describe the athlete's attributes (e.g., skills, attitude, physicality, that special *something*).

69.

At this moment in your career, what's your primary weakness as an athlete? When asked to name a weakness, some athletes identified the following:

Nervous	Insecure	Frightened	Weak
Timid	Unreliable	Unhealthy	Unfocused
Hot-tempered	Unfocused	Lazy	Disorganized
Know-it-all	Negative	Whiner	Inconsistent

Write about your primary weakness as an athlete and what you plan to do to correct this challenge.

70.

Write about the times in your athletic career when you have witnessed the following behaviors, traits, or actions by an athlete, coach, fan, opponent, or official:

Courage:

Unselfishness:

Cruelty:

Stupidity:

Arrogance:

Humility:

Insensitivity:

Forgiveness:

Danger:

Kindness:

Dishonesty:

71.

Dream up 5 journal prompts for athletes and share them with me. Email the prompts to rich.kent@maine.edu

1.

2.

3.

4.

5.

Try one of your prompts:

72.

"Writing organizes and clarifies our thoughts. Writing is how we think our way into a subject and make it our own. Writing enables us to find out what we know—and what we don't know—about whatever we're trying to learn." –William Zinsser

In what ways has this quotation proven true for you as an athlete who has kept a journal ?

PRESEASON REFLECTIONS

Preseason Reflections

What were your strengths last season as an athlete?

Last season, in what areas did your skills need to improve?

In the offseason, what did you do to improve as an athlete?

Write about and describe your most satisfying performance last season. What contributed to this performance?

Write about and describe your most disappointing performance from last season. What contributed to this performance?

If you're on a team...

Last year our team strengths included the following:

Last year our team needed to work more in the following areas:

Write about and describe the most satisfying team performance last season. What contributed to this performance?

Write about and describe the most disappointing team performance from last season. What contributed to this performance?

What do you believe this year's team strengths will be?

In what areas will this year's team need to improve?

Final Thoughts:

What is your prediction for the team in the upcoming season?

MIDSEASON REFLECTIONS

Midseason Reflections

What are your strengths so far this season as an athlete?

In what areas do you need to improve?

What's your most significant accomplishment so far this season?

Write about your best personal performance so far this season. What contributed to your success?

Write about your worst performance so far this season. What contributed to your poor play? How did you rebound from that performance?

If you're on a team…

So far this season our team strengths include…

Our team needs to improve in the following areas…

Midseason Letter

Write a letter about your performance thus far to your coach, a teammate…
or to *yourself*.

POSTSEASON REFLECTIONS

Postseason Reflections

What have been your strengths this season as an athlete?

What areas still need improvement?

What has been your most significant accomplishment this season?

Write about your best personal performance this season. What contributed to your success?

Write about your worst performance this season. What contributed to this performance? How did you rebound from that performance?

If you're on a team...

This season our team strengths included...

Our team still needed to work on the following areas...

What are your plans in the offseason for training?

COMPETITION ANALYSES

Competition Analysis

Date: _____ Opponent/Competition: _____
Place: _____ Result: _____

My strengths as an athlete in the competition:

My weaknesses as an athlete in the competition:

Team strengths in the competition:

Team weaknesses in the competition:

Opponent's strengths:

Opponent's weaknesses:

What do you believe was the "difference" in the competition? What helped you do well or what seemed to hinder your performance today?

What adjustments might you make for your next competition?

Other comments about strategy, attitude, preparation:

Competition Analysis

Date: _____ Opponent/Competition: _____
Place: _____ Result: _____

My strengths as an athlete in the competition:

My weaknesses as an athlete in the competition:

Team strengths in the competition:

Team weaknesses in the competition:

Opponent's strengths:

Opponent's weaknesses:

What do you believe was the "difference" in the competition? What helped you do well or what seemed to hinder your performance today?

What adjustments might you make for your next competition?

Other comments about strategy, attitude, preparation:

Competition Analysis

Date: _____ Opponent/Competition: _____
Place: _____ Result: _____

My strengths as an athlete in the competition:

My weaknesses as an athlete in the competition:

Team strengths in the competition:

Team weaknesses in the competition:

Opponent's strengths:

Opponent's weaknesses:

What do you believe was the "difference" in the competition? What helped you do well or what seemed to hinder your performance today?

What adjustments might you make for your next competition?

Other comments about strategy, attitude, preparation:

Competition Analysis

Date: _____ Opponent/Competition: _____
Place: _____ Result: _____

My strengths as an athlete in the competition:

My weaknesses as an athlete in the competition:

Team strengths in the competition:

Team weaknesses in the competition:

Opponent's strengths:

Opponent's weaknesses:

What do you believe was the "difference" in the competition? What helped you do well or what seemed to hinder your performance today?

What adjustments might you make for your next competition?

Other comments about strategy, attitude, preparation:

Competition Analysis

Date: _____ Opponent/Competition: _____
Place: _____ Result: _____

My strengths as an athlete in the competition:

My weaknesses as an athlete in the competition:

Team strengths in the competition:

Team weaknesses in the competition:

Opponent's strengths:

Opponent's weaknesses:

What do you believe was the "difference" in the competition? What helped you do well or what seemed to hinder your performance today?

What adjustments might you make for your next competition?

Other comments about strategy, attitude, preparation:

Competition Analysis

Date: _____ Opponent/Competition: _____
Place: _____ Result: _____

My strengths as an athlete in the competition:

My weaknesses as an athlete in the competition:

Team strengths in the competition:

Team weaknesses in the competition:

Opponent's strengths:

Opponent's weaknesses:

What do you believe was the "difference" in the competition? What helped you do well or what seemed to hinder your performance today?

What adjustments might you make for your next competition?

Other comments about strategy, attitude, preparation:

Competition Analysis

Date: _____ Opponent/Competition: _____

Place: _____ Result: _____

My strengths as an athlete in the competition:

My weaknesses as an athlete in the competition:

Team strengths in the competition:

Team weaknesses in the competition:

Opponent's strengths:

Opponent's weaknesses:

What do you believe was the "difference" in the competition? What helped you do well or what seemed to hinder your performance today?

What adjustments might you make for your next competition?

Other comments about strategy, attitude, preparation:

Competition Analysis

Date: _____ Opponent/Competition: _____
Place: _____ Result: _____

My strengths as an athlete in the competition:

My weaknesses as an athlete in the competition:

Team strengths in the competition:

Team weaknesses in the competition:

Opponent's strengths:

Opponent's weaknesses:

What do you believe was the "difference" in the competition? What helped you do well or what seemed to hinder your performance today?

What adjustments might you make for your next competition?

Other comments about strategy, attitude, preparation:

Competition Analysis

Date: _____ Opponent/Competition: _____
Place: _____ Result: _____

My strengths as an athlete in the competition:

My weaknesses as an athlete in the competition:

Team strengths in the competition:

Team weaknesses in the competition:

Opponent's strengths:

Opponent's weaknesses:

What do you believe was the "difference" in the competition? What helped you do well or what seemed to hinder your performance today?

What adjustments might you make for your next competition?

Other comments about strategy, attitude, preparation:

Competition Analysis

Date: _____ Opponent/Competition: _____

Place: _____ Result: _____

My strengths as an athlete in the competition:

My weaknesses as an athlete in the competition:

Team strengths in the competition:

Team weaknesses in the competition:

Opponent's strengths:

Opponent's weaknesses:

What do you believe was the "difference" in the competition? What helped you do well or what seemed to hinder your performance today?

What adjustments might you make for your next competition?

Other comments about strategy, attitude, preparation:

Competition Analysis

Date: _____ Opponent/Competition: _____
Place: _____ Result: _____

My strengths as an athlete in the competition:

My weaknesses as an athlete in the competition:

Team strengths in the competition:

Team weaknesses in the competition:

Opponent's strengths:

Opponent's weaknesses:

What do you believe was the "difference" in the competition? What helped you do well or what seemed to hinder your performance today?

What adjustments might you make for your next competition?

Other comments about strategy, attitude, preparation:

Competition Analysis

Date: _____ Opponent/Competition: _____
Place: _____ Result: _____

My strengths as an athlete in the competition:

My weaknesses as an athlete in the competition:

Team strengths in the competition:

Team weaknesses in the competition:

Opponent's strengths:

Opponent's weaknesses:

What do you believe was the "difference" in the competition? What helped you do well or what seemed to hinder your performance today?

What adjustments might you make for your next competition?

Other comments about strategy, attitude, preparation:

Competition Analysis

Date: _____ Opponent/Competition: _____

Place: _____ Result: _____

My strengths as an athlete in the competition:

My weaknesses as an athlete in the competition:

Team strengths in the competition:

Team weaknesses in the competition:

Opponent's strengths:

Opponent's weaknesses:

What do you believe was the "difference" in the competition? What helped you do well or what seemed to hinder your performance today?

What adjustments might you make for your next competition?

Other comments about strategy, attitude, preparation:

Competition Analysis

Date: _____ Opponent/Competition: _____

Place: _____ Result: _____

My strengths as an athlete in the competition:

My weaknesses as an athlete in the competition:

Team strengths in the competition:

Team weaknesses in the competition:

Opponent's strengths:

Opponent's weaknesses:

What do you believe was the "difference" in the competition? What helped you do well or what seemed to hinder your performance today?

What adjustments might you make for your next competition?

Other comments about strategy, attitude, preparation:

Competition Analysis

Date: _____ Opponent/Competition: _____

Place: _____ Result: _____

My strengths as an athlete in the competition:

My weaknesses as an athlete in the competition:

Team strengths in the competition:

Team weaknesses in the competition:

Opponent's strengths:

Opponent's weaknesses:

What do you believe was the "difference" in the competition? What helped you do well or what seemed to hinder your performance today?

What adjustments might you make for your next competition?

Other comments about strategy, attitude, preparation:

Competition Analysis

Date: _____ Opponent/Competition: _____
Place: _____ Result: _____

My strengths as an athlete in the competition:

My weaknesses as an athlete in the competition:

Team strengths in the competition:

Team weaknesses in the competition:

Opponent's strengths:

Opponent's weaknesses:

What do you believe was the "difference" in the competition? What helped you do well or what seemed to hinder your performance today?

What adjustments might you make for your next competition?

Other comments about strategy, attitude, preparation:

Competition Analysis

Date: _____ Opponent/Competition: _____
Place: _____ Result: _____

My strengths as an athlete in the competition:

My weaknesses as an athlete in the competition:

Team strengths in the competition:

Team weaknesses in the competition:

Opponent's strengths:

Opponent's weaknesses:

What do you believe was the "difference" in the competition? What helped you do well or what seemed to hinder your performance today?

What adjustments might you make for your next competition?

Other comments about strategy, attitude, preparation:

Competition Analysis

Date: _____ Opponent/Competition: _____

Place: _____ Result: _____

My strengths as an athlete in the competition:

My weaknesses as an athlete in the competition:

Team strengths in the competition:

Team weaknesses in the competition:

Opponent's strengths:

Opponent's weaknesses:

What do you believe was the "difference" in the competition? What helped you do well or what seemed to hinder your performance today?

What adjustments might you make for your next competition?

Other comments about strategy, attitude, preparation:

Competition Analysis

Date: _____ Opponent/Competition: _____
Place: _____ Result: _____

My strengths as an athlete in the competition:

My weaknesses as an athlete in the competition:

Team strengths in the competition:

Team weaknesses in the competition:

Opponent's strengths:

Opponent's weaknesses:

What do you believe was the "difference" in the competition? What helped you do well or what seemed to hinder your performance today?

What adjustments might you make for your next competition?

Other comments about strategy, attitude, preparation:

Competition Analysis

Date: _____ Opponent/Competition: _____

Place: _____ Result: _____

My strengths as an athlete in the competition:

My weaknesses as an athlete in the competition:

Team strengths in the competition:

Team weaknesses in the competition:

Opponent's strengths:

Opponent's weaknesses:

What do you believe was the "difference" in the competition? What helped you do well or what seemed to hinder your performance today?

What adjustments might you make for your next competition?

Other comments about strategy, attitude, preparation:

ADDITIONAL JOURNAL PAGES

Journal # _____

Journal # _____

Journal # _____

Journal # _____

Journal # _____

Journal # _____

Journal # _____

Journal # _____

Journal # _____

Journal # ____

Journal # _____

Journal # _____

Journal # _____

ABOUT THE AUTHOR

RICHARD KENT is a professor at the University of Maine and the director of the Maine Writing Project, a site of the National Writing Project. The author of many books, including *Writing on the Bus*, *The Athlete's Workbook*, and *Soccer Team Notebook*, Kent is a consultant to teams and athletes across the United States. He has coached at different levels over the past four decades.

For more about athletes' journals and team notebooks, checkout Kent's resource website: WritingAthletes.com

Write. Learn. Perform.

Made in the USA
San Bernardino, CA
13 December 2016